SANTA MONICA
PUBLIC
LIBRARY

www.smpl.org

4-WEEK LOAN

TELEPHONE RENEWALS:
Main Library. 451-1866
Ocean Park Branch. 392-3804
Fairview Branch 450-0443
Montana Branch 829-7081

DATE DUE

OCT 14 2003	
DEC - 2 2004	
APR 21 2005	
JUN 30 2005	

Chickenpox

Dr. Alvin Silverstein,

Virginia Silverstein, and

Laura Silverstein Nunn

My Health

Franklin Watts

A Division of Grolier Publishing

New York • London • Hong Kong • Sydney

Danbury, Connecticut

Photographs©: Custom Medical Stock Photo: 25 bottom (Dr. P. Marazzi/SPL), 8 (Lynn Sechler), 39; Peter Arnold Inc.: 32 (Leonard Lessin); Photo Researchers: 11 (Biophoto Associates/SS), 18 (Grapes/Michaud), 34 (Aaron Haupt), 21, 25 top (Dr. P. Marazzi/SPL), 13 (Oliver Meckes/Gelderblom), 4, 9 (SPL), 16 (Dept.of Medical Photography, St. Stephen's Hospital,London/SPL); PhotoEdit: 29 (Robert Brenner), 36 (Myrleen Cate), 23, 35 (Tony Freeman), 37 (Michael Newman); Stock Boston: 30 (Spencer Grant), 31 (Brent Jones); Stone: 20 (Pascal Crapet), 22, 24 (David C. Tomlinson); Visuals Unlimited: 27 (Bill Beatty), 6 (Tom Edwards), 28 (Ken Greer).

Medical illustration by Leonard Morgan
Cartoons by Rick Stromoski

> Visit Franklin Watts on the Internet at:
> http://publishing.grolier.com

Library of Congress Cataloging-in-Publication Data

Silverstein, Alvin.
    Chickenpox / by Alvin Silverstein, Virginia Silverstein, and Laura Silverstein Nunn.
        p.   cm.—(My Health)
    Includes bibliographical references and index.
    Summary: Describes what chickenpox is, how the body fights this disease, how it is spread, symptoms, treatment, and new vaccinations to prevent chickenpox.
        ISBN 0-531-11782-0 (lib. bdg.)   0-531-13970-0 (pbk.)
        1. Chickenpox—Juvenile literature. [1. Chickenpox. 2. Diseases.]
I. Silverstein, Virginia B. II. Nunn, Laura Silverstein. III. Title. IV. Series.
RC125.S549   2001
616.9'14—dc21   00-027344

Printed in the United States of America
    2 3 4 5 6 7 8 9 10 R 10 09 08 07 06 05 04 03 02

GROLIER
PUBLISHING

Contents

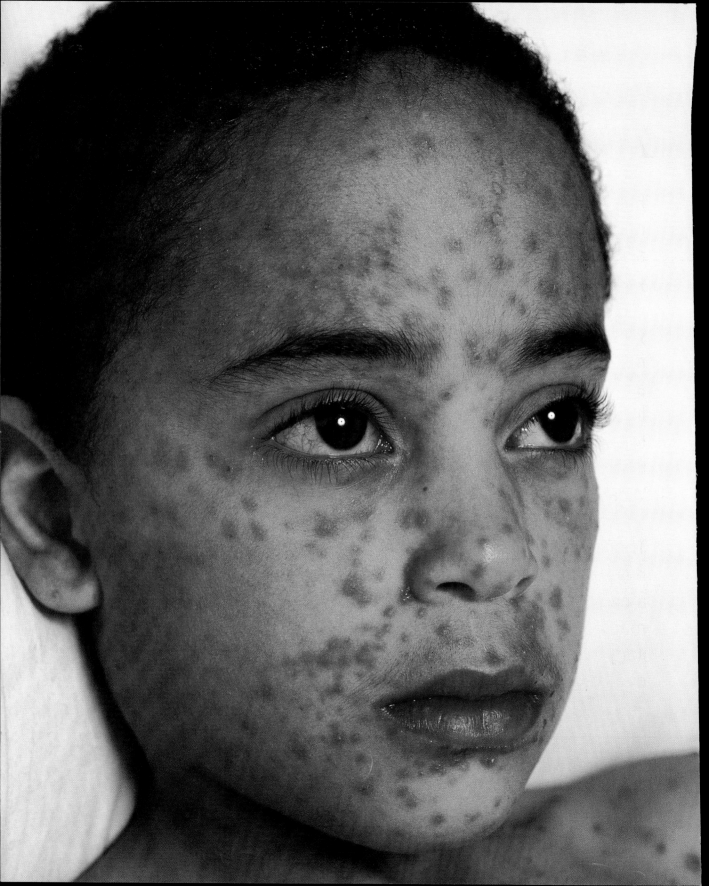

An Itchy Illness

For the last few days, you haven't been feeling quite right. You've had a runny nose and a cough. You've also been feeling more tired than usual. It seems like you probably have a cold.

Then you wake up one morning and drag yourself into the bathroom. You look into the mirror with bleary eyes and see red spots all over your face! Where did they come from? They look a little bit like mosquito bites. Then you notice more of them on your stomach and arms. What's going on?

What you have is not a cold. Those red spots tell the tale—you have chickenpox! Chickenpox is a common illness that affects many kids. It causes red, itchy blisters to pop up all over your body.

Did You Know...

Chickenpox actually has nothing to do with chickens. The name chickenpox comes from cicer (CHICK-er), a Latin word for chickpeas.

People used to think that the red bumps that appear when someone has chickenpox look like chickpeas.

◄ **What are all those red spots? Chickenpox!**

Chickenpox is common in children between 5 and 9 years old.

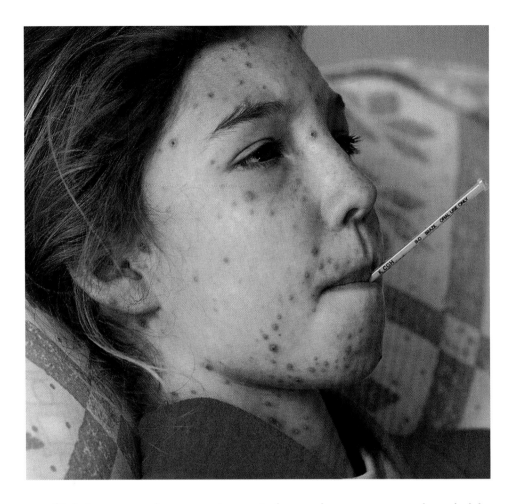

Chickenpox is easy to catch and can spread quickly through families, schools, and day-care centers. About 4 million people get chickenpox each year in, the United States. Anyone can get chickenpox, but chickenpox is most common in children between the ages of 5 and 9. About 90 percent of all chickenpox cases occur in children under the age of 15.

Other Itchy Illnesses

Chickenpox is not the only childhood disease that causes an itchy rash, but it is the most common one. Some of these other itchy illnesses are also caused by a virus, but it is fairly easy to tell them apart by looking at the rashes. Chickenpox is the only disease that causes a blistery rash.

- Measles is caused by a virus and produces a reddish-brown, blotchy rash.
- Rubella is caused by a virus and produces a rash made up of small pink dots. It is sometimes called German measles.
- Scarlet fever is caused by a bacterium and produces a pinkish-red rash with a high fever headache, and a sore throat. A child's tongue usually looks white with red spots.
- Roseola infantum is caused by a virus and produces a rosy red rash. It usually affects very young children.
- Fifth disease is caused by a virus. It produces a bright red rash on a child's cheeks, followed by a lacy red rash on the arms, legs, stomach, and back. It is also called slapped-cheek disease.

Chickenpox is usually a fairly mild illness. Most people can get better in less than 2 weeks without taking any medicine. But having chickenpox can make you feel miserable. Those itchy blisters can be really uncomfortable.

What causes chickenpox? How can you relieve the itching if you do get it? If you haven't had chickenpox yet, is there any way to avoid it? Let's find out what chickenpox is all about.

Chickenpox can make you feel miserable.

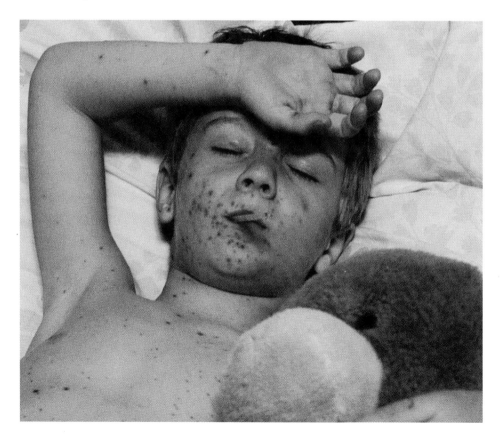

What Is Chickenpox?

Chickenpox is an illness that produces a rash of red, itchy blisters all over your body. It is caused by tiny germs called **viruses**. Viruses are so small that you need a powerful microscope to see them. The virus that causes chickenpox is called the **varicella-zoster virus**. It is so small that thousands of them can fit on the head of a pin.

Viruses are tiny. These chickenpox viruses have been magnified more than 96,800 times.

Activity 1: Gotcha!

One reason chickenpox is so easy to catch is that just touching the material that oozes out of an infected blister can spread the germs.

Put some liquid vegetable dye in a bowl. (Use wild colors like purple, blue, or green.) Dip your fingers in the bowl to wet them with the dye. Now do some normal things, like eating a snack or bouncing a ball or drawing a picture. Every few minutes, dip your fingers in the bowl with the dye again.

After 15 minutes, look at yourself in a mirror. How many times did you touch your face? You'll be able to tell because you will have colored spots from the vegetable dye on your skin. What else did you touch?

You probably didn't realize how often you touch your face without even thinking about it. Now can you imagine how hard it is to keep from spreading chickenpox viruses?

Viruses can live only inside an animal or a plant. The viruses that cause chickenpox live in the soft, wet lining inside a person's nose and throat. They invade the cells that make up this lining and force the cells to make more viruses. When a cell is full of new viruses, it bursts open and the viruses spill out.

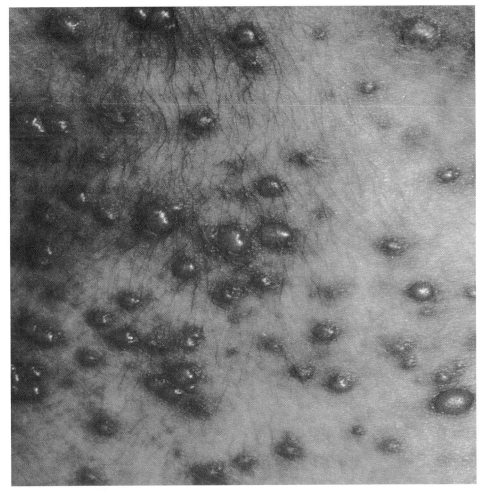

When chickenpox viruses invade your body, a blistery rash develops.

Some of the viruses are carried out of the body in **mucus**—the wet, slimy liquid that moistens the linings of the nose and the throat. Other viruses pass into the blood and tissues and are carried to other parts of the body. They invade and damage other kinds of body cells and take control of them too. When chickenpox viruses multiply inside a person's skin cells, a blistery rash appears on the skin.

A few viruses may even invade nerve cells. These viruses do not multiply. Instead, they lay low and hide out. They may stay inactive for many years. During this time, they do not make you sick.

Did You Know...

Some chickenpox blisters are as small as a pencil eraser. Others are as large as a dime.

How Your Body Defends Itself

People often get sick when tiny germs invade their bodies, but our bodies have many defenses against germs. As soon as a virus attacks, cells send out chemical alarm signals. These signals tell the body that the cells are in trouble. Some of these chemicals make a watery liquid leak out of tiny blood vessels. When the liquid seeps into surrounding tissues, the entire area becomes swollen. We say that the area is **inflamed**.

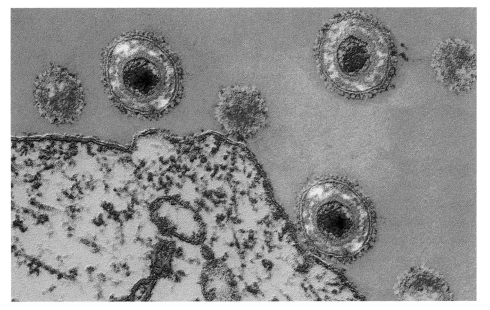

These round chickenpox viruses are attacking a body cell.

13

The Dangers of Chickenpox

Chickenpox is often a more serious disease in teens and adults. They get more pocks, and the illness usually lasts longer. Chickenpox can be dangerous to newborn babies and pregnant women.

Chickenpox can be very dangerous for people with cancer or AIDS because their immune system is too weak to fight off the virus. Each year, chickenpox sends about 9,000 people to the hospital. This normally mild disease causes 50 to 100 deaths each year.

Meanwhile, other chemicals call in the body's defending soldiers—the **white blood cells**. White blood cells are always on guard against germs and other invaders that can make you sick. They swim through your blood and can squeeze through the spaces between body cells. They can move easily through inflamed tissues.

White blood cells are part of your **immune system**. You have several kinds of white blood cells. Each kind has its own important job. Some white blood cells attack and kill germs. Others produce special chemicals called **antibodies**.

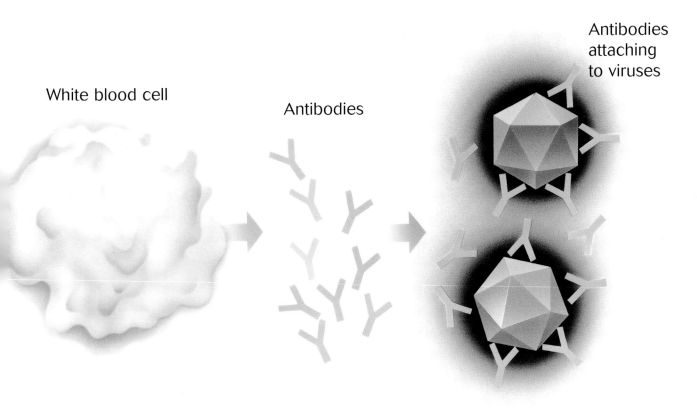

White blood cell

Antibodies

Antibodies attaching to viruses

When viruses invade your body, some white blood cells produce antibodies. The antibodies attach to the viruses and help destroy them.

Antibodies are like ammunition for the white cell soldiers. They attach to viruses and stop them from attacking body cells. An antibody fits into a virus like a key fits into a lock. Some antibodies kill germs themselves. Others make it easier for white blood cells to destroy the virus.

After the battle against chickenpox is over, your body keeps a supply of antibodies ready. If the chickenpox virus enters your body again, the antibodies will be ready to fight. They will destroy the new viruses before they have a chance to do much damage. That's why most people get chickenpox only once.

However, as a person gets older, the immune system becomes less able to fight off germs. Illnesses such as AIDS or cancer can also weaken the body's defenses. If a person has a weakened immune system, the inactive chickenpox viruses hiding inside nerve cells may become active. If these cells multiply, the person may get a disease called **shingles**. Most cases of shingles occur in people over the age of 50.

The shingles rash follows the path of a nerve infected with the chickenpox virus. It may look like a red band.

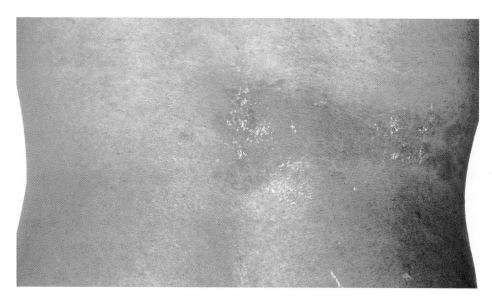

Both chickenpox and shingles produce a rash. The chickenpox rash is usually very itchy. The shingles rash is often very painful—probably because the viruses are in the nerve cells that carry pain messages.

Unlike chickenpox, shingles is not **contagious**. No one catches shingles directly from someone who has it. However, because the shingles rash contains the active chickenpox virus, a person who has never had chickenpox can catch it from a person who has shingles.

Did You Know...

The shingles rash often forms a narrow band that looks like a belt. That is why the word "shingles" comes from a Latin word that means "belt." The name of this disease has nothing to do with the shingles on a roof.

How Does Chickenpox Spread?

Have you ever heard someone say, "Cover your mouth when you sneeze!"? That's because sneezing can spread the germs that cause a cold. Everybody knows

Achoo! Sneezing can spread chickenpox germs.

that colds are easy to catch. Chickenpox is easy to catch too.

Like colds, chickenpox is contagious. It can spread easily from one person to another. Viruses leave the body of an **infected** person and get inside the body of a healthy person. A person who has never had chickenpox will get the disease after being exposed to it.

When you get sick, virus particles hide in the mucus in your nose and throat. But how do these viruses leave your body and find a new home in someone else's body? Some viruses can spread through the air. When you sneeze or cough—or even when you talk—tiny droplets of moisture spray out of your nose and mouth. Chickenpox viruses can ride on those tiny droplets.

Did You Know...

Most cases of chickenpox happen during the late winter and early spring. That's because people stay inside with the doors and windows closed during cold weather, and they spend a lot of time with other people who can pass it along.

Chickenpox may also be spread by hands. If you wipe your nose or cough into your hand, the virus particles get on your hands. If you touch somebody else's hand, you pass on some of your chickenpox germs. The virus

particles do not get into the body through the skin on the fingers, but they can get in when people put their fingers to their mouth or nose. You can also pick up germs by touching an object that was recently touched by somebody with chickenpox. People can leave germs on doorknobs, telephones, dishes, books, toys, money, and other common objects.

The liquid inside chickenpox blisters can also spread the disease. The liquid contains virus particles. If you scratch the blisters, the liquid will ooze out. Anybody who touches this liquid can get the disease. Chickenpox germs may even be left on clothes and bedsheets that were in contact with the oozing blisters.

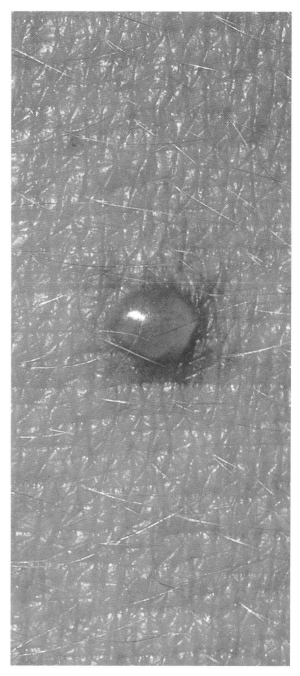

A chickenpox blister, like this one, is filled with liquid containing lots of chickenpox germs.

Don't Scratch that Itch!

The chickenpox rash can get pretty itchy. All you want to do is scratch, but don't do it! The **scab** covering a blister has an important job. It helps keep out germs while the damaged tissues are healing. If this protective covering is broken, germs can get into the blister and start to multiply, producing another infection. This may leave a **scar**, or pockmark, on your skin. If left alone, pocks will heal and gradually fade away. It may take up to a year for all the pocks to disappear completely.

Some of these chickenpox blisters have formed scabs that will help them heal.

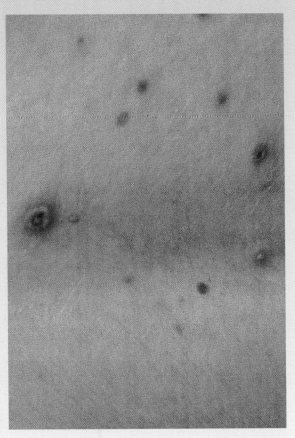

Since chickenpox is so easy to catch, doctors usually prefer to diagnose kids over the phone rather than in person. They do not want other patients in their waiting room to get chickenpox too. A visit to the doctor is necessary only if you have serious itching or if your rash causes pain.

Spotting the Signs

The chickenpox rash may be easy to spot, but you could have the disease and not even know it! Those red, itchy pocks are usually not the *first* signs of chickenpox.

Many kids get a fever, sore throat, and swollen lymph nodes before a rash appears. These signs develop 10 to 21 days after contact with the virus. The rash usually appears a couple of days later.

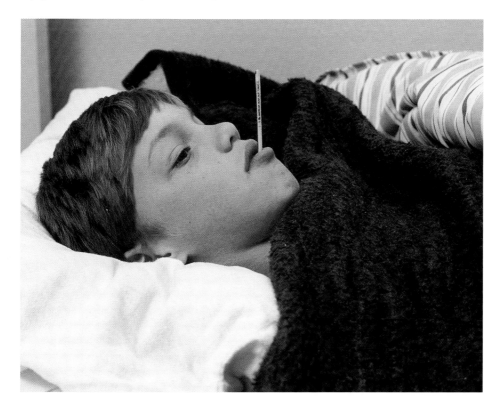

You may feel sick a few days before you see the chickenpox rash.

The rash usually develops first on the chest, back, or scalp. Then it spreads to the rest of your body. Soon there are spots on your face, arms, legs, and armpits. Most people get between 100 to 200 pocks.

Can you count the number of pocks on this boy's back?

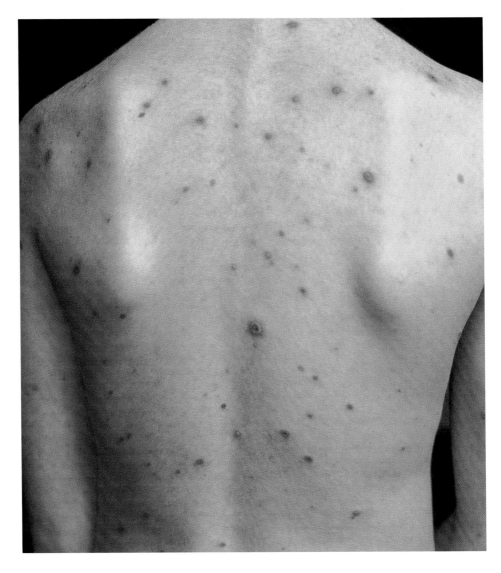

Some people get a very mild case of chickenpox. They may have just a few blisters on their body. Other people are covered from head to toe with the rash. Pocks appear on their eyes and tongue. They may get as many as 500 blisters.

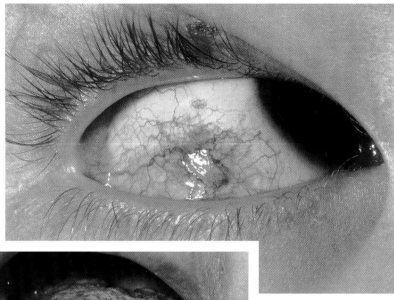

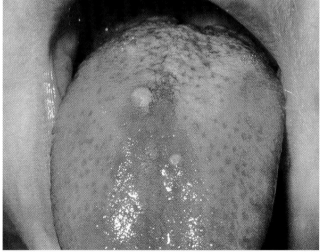

Getting a pock on your eyeball (above) or tongue (left) can be really rough.

All in the Family

Children who catch chickenpox from a brother or sister often have a more serious and more widespread rash than children who catch it from a classmate at school. That's because the more someone is exposed to the chickenpox virus, the worse the symptoms are.

Each pock goes through different stages of development. It starts out as a flat red area. Then it develops into a raised red bump. The bump soon changes into a clear blister, which then turns cloudy as **pus** gathers inside. Eventually, a dry crust or scab forms over the blister. The whole process from red spot to scabbed-over blister takes only a few hours. New pocks continue to appear and develop. By the second day of the rash, a person may have pocks in all different stages.

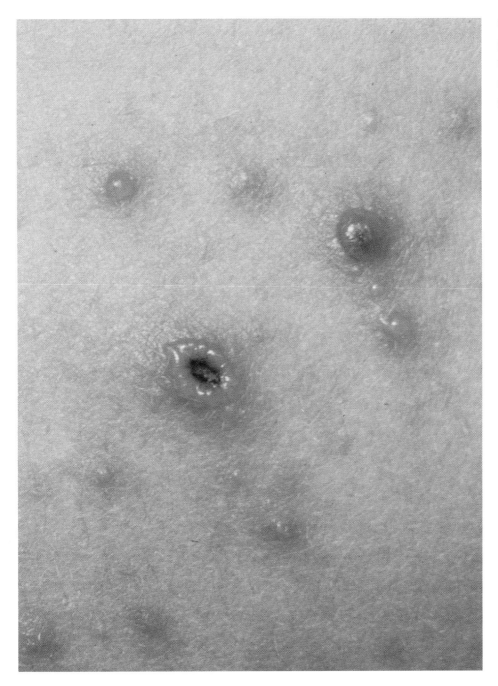

Older pocks get scabs while new ones are forming.

Signs of a Battle

Inside each pock, a battle rages between the virus invaders and the body's defenders. Your white blood cells work hard to attack and destroy the viruses, but some are poisoned by all the germs they have eaten and die. The whitish pus that forms in chickenpox blisters is made up of the bodies of dead white blood cells.

The pus in chickenpox blisters contains dead white blood cells.

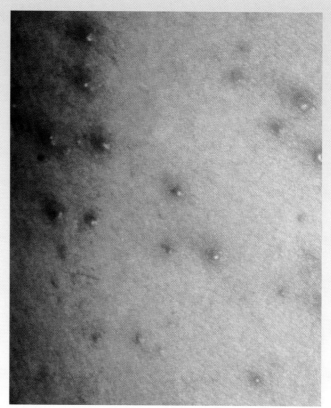

A person with chickenpox is contagious for about 5 or 7 days—from 1 to 2 days before the first pocks appear until all the blisters have crusted over. Because people are contagious before they even feel sick, it is very easy to spread chickenpox. Doctors say that kids who have chickenpox should not go to school for at least 5 days after the first pock appears.

Treating Chickenpox

There is no cure for chickenpox, but there are things you can do to ease the itching. Try taking a bath in cool or warm water containing some uncooked oatmeal, baking soda, or cornstarch. Don't soak in a hot bath—the heat will just make you itch more. You can also hold a cool compress against the really itchy areas.

Calamine lotion and anti-itch allergy drugs can also help control the itching. If these remedies don't help

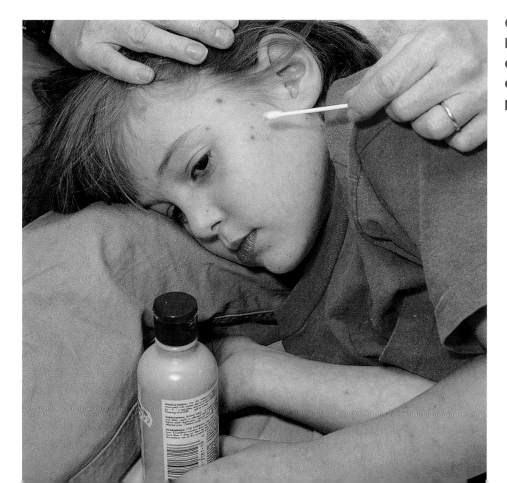

Calamine lotion can ease the itch of chickenpox blisters.

and you can't stop scratching, try covering your hands with gloves or socks and keep your fingernails cut very short. This will prevent you from scratching the crust off your blisters.

If you have blisters in your mouth, you may have trouble eating and drinking. Stick to cold drinks and soft, bland foods such as gelatin. Stay away from anything that is highly acidic, such as orange juice. To soothe the sores in your mouth and throat, gargle with water that has a half teaspoon of salt mixed in.

Vitamin Magic

Some medical experts say extra vitamin C in your diet can help keep you healthy. They believe that vitamin C makes your immune system stronger. Oranges are good sources of vitamin C. But if you have sores in your mouth and throat, orange juice might sting. You could take vitamin C pills or drink carrot or tomato juice. They are also rich in vitamin A, which may also help the immune system.

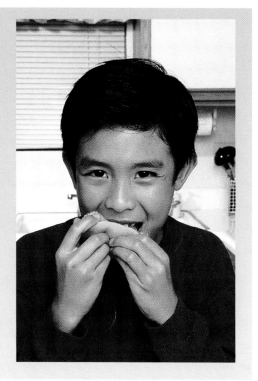

Oranges are rich in vitamin C, which can help to keep you healthy.

Chickenpox and Aspirin Don't Mix

Children with chickenpox should not take aspirin. It can lead to **Reye's syndrome**, a serious or even deadly disease that affects the liver and brain. Doctors used to see many cases of Reye's syndrome in children who took aspirin to treat chickenpox symptoms. Now that doctors advise parents not to give aspirin to children with viruses, Reye's syndrome is very rare.

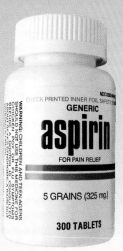

Children with chickenpox should not take aspirin.

Besides itchy blisters, you may also have a high fever. Cool baths can help to lower a fever. You could also try taking a pain reliever with acetaminophen (uh-SEE-tuh-MIN-uh-fin). One common example is Tylenol. Don't forget to check the label—or check with your doctor—to make sure you are taking the right amount.

Doctors don't like to give medicine to people with an illness that is normally mild. Medicine may cause allergic reactions or bad side effects in some people. Also, when a medicine is used too often, germs that are not killed by the drug may multiply and spread to other people. Then the drug can no longer kill the germs.

That's why most healthcare workers believe that chickenpox should be allowed to run its course without the use of any medications. Normally, home remedies are enough to relieve the itching and fever. However, in 1992, the United States government approved medicine called **acyclovir** (ay-SYE-clo-veer) to treat chickenpox.

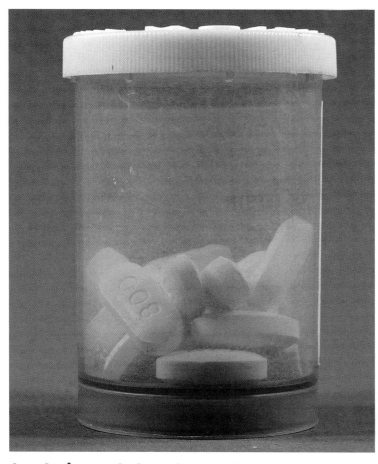

Acyclovir may help to lessen the symptoms of chickenpox.

Acyclovir prevents viruses from multiplying. When it is taken within 24 hours after the first few pocks appear, the disease is much milder than usual. The rash goes away much more quickly, and there are fewer sores.

This drug sounds like a great way to reduce the miserable symptoms of chickenpox. So why don't more people use it? Acyclovir helps only if it is given in the very early stages of the disease. It is also expensive and may not be easy to take. (It works best when it is injected rather than taken as pills.)

Acyclovir should be used only for the people who are at risk for developing serious complications—newborn babies, teens, adults, and people who have weakened immune systems. For them, chickenpox can be very dangerous. Treating them with medication is necessary.

Protecting Against Chickenpox

If you have chickenpox, there are lots of things you can do to keep from spreading the disease. First of all, try to stay away from people who have not had chickenpox. This disease is so contagious that you can spread it just by talking to a friend or sharing food.

It is also important to wash your hands many times throughout the day. If you wipe your nose, sneeze,

Washing your hands frequently can help to stop chickenpox germs from spreading.

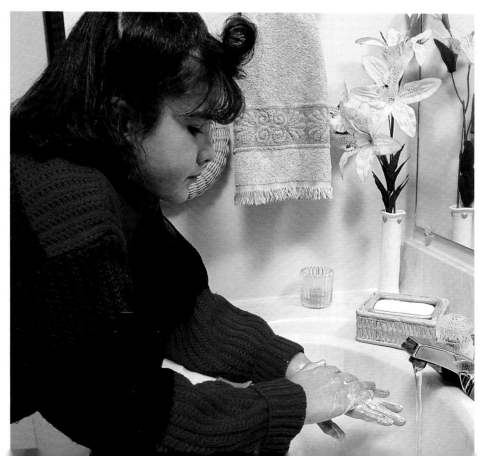

yawn, or accidentally break open a chickenpox blister, you may get virus particles on your hands.

If the liquids from blisters or mucus get on your bedsheets, towels, and clothes, other people who touch these items may get chickenpox. Be sure to wash sheets, towels, and clothes in hot, soapy water to get rid of any germs.

To get rid of viruses on clothes and bedding that came in contact with chickenpox sores, wash them in hot, soapy water.

When a high-risk individual, such as a newborn baby, a pregnant woman, or a person with a weakened immune system, is exposed to someone with chickenpox, a simple illness can turn into a deadly disease. To prevent this from happening, a doctor may give the person a shot that contains antibodies to the chickenpox virus. This will protect the person from the virus, but it is only temporary. For the treatment to work, the patient must receive it within 96 hours after exposure to the virus.

A pregnant woman should try to stay away from people with chickenpox. If she is exposed, she can get a shot containing antibodies.

In 1995, **Varivax**—a **vaccine** to protect people against chickenpox—was approved by the United States government. Chickenpox is the last of the major childhood diseases. Vaccines for polio, measles, mumps, and rubella have been around for many years. When a person is injected with the vaccine, he or she produces antibodies against the virus without actually getting the disease. Most of the people who have received the vaccine will not catch chickenpox even if they are exposed to the virus.

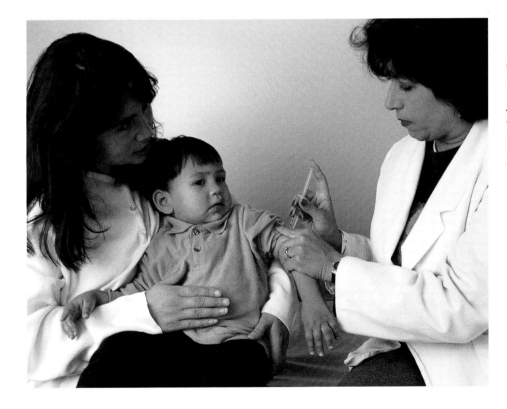

Now kids can be protected against chickenpox just like the other childhood diseases.

Activity 2: Who's Had Chickenpox?

Take a survey of your friends and relatives to find out whether the chickenpox vaccine is making a big difference. Talk to as many people as you can. Be sure to include males and females, people with different cultural backgrounds, and people of different ages.

1. Have you ever had chickenpox? If so,
   - How old were you when you had it?
   - Do you know who spread it to you?
   - What kind of symptoms did you have?
   - Were the symptoms mild or serious?
   - Do you have any pockmarks?
2. Did you get the chickenpox vaccine? If so,
   - How old were you at the time?

Make a table of your results. You will probably find that most teens and adults have had chickenpox. The vaccine was approved in 1995, so children born after that may never have the disease.

The American Academy of Pediatrics recommends that children 12 to 18 months old should get one shot of Varivax. They may receive it at the same time that they receive their measles-mumps-rubella shot. Children 18 months to 12 years old who have not had chickenpox should get one shot of the vaccine. Teens and adults who have not had chickenpox or a vaccination should get two shots of the vaccine 4 to 8 weeks apart.

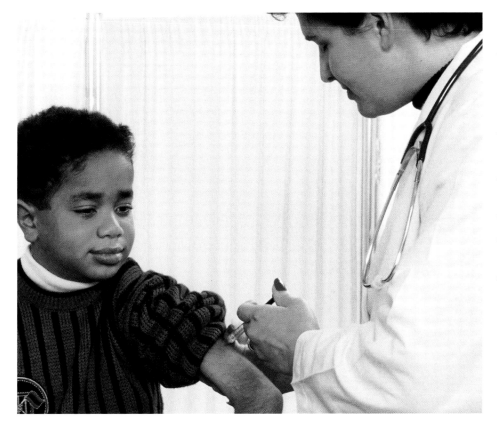

Most vaccines are given to very young children, but since the chickenpox vaccine has not been around very long, it is also given to school-aged kids, teens, and adults.

The chickenpox vaccine is 70 to 90 percent effective in preventing the disease. This isn't as good as the measles vaccine, which protects about 97 percent of those who receive it. But studies have shown that people who develop chickenpox after receiving the vaccine usually get a milder case than people who have not been vaccinated.

Because the chickenpox vaccine is so new, doctors don't know yet how long it will protect people from chickenpox. The vaccines against some diseases are good for a lifetime, but others provide protection for only a few years. This worries some people because chickenpox can be very serious in adults. If it turns out that people need further protection, doctors will be ready to give patients booster shots.

Health experts hope that the Varivax vaccine will help protect people in high-risk groups by greatly reducing the number of people with active chickenpox. For everyone else, the vaccine could mean the end to an irritating childhood disease.

Gl●ssary

acyclovir—a drug used to treat chickenpox

antibody—a special germ-fighting chemical produced by white blood cells

contagious—easily spread from one person to another

immune system—the body's disease-fighting system. It includes white blood cells, which protect against foreign invaders.

infect—to invade and damage body tissues

inflamed—body tissue that is swollen because it is damaged. An inflamed area may look red, feel warm, and cause pain.

mucus—a gooey liquid produced by cells in the lining of the nose and throat

pus—a thick, yellow material that comes out of an infected wound

Reye's syndrome—a rare but serious illness that is associated with taking aspirin during a viral infection

scab—a dry crust that forms over a sore or wound for protection while it heals

scar—a mark that is left on the skin after a cut or sore heals. Chickenpox usually leaves scars only when the sores are infected by bacteria.

shingles—an illness that produces a painful skin rash. It occurs when the chickenpox virus is reactivated.

vaccine—a substance that stimulates the body to form protective antibodies against a particular kind of disease germ

varicella-zoster virus—the virus that causes chickenpox

Varivax—a vaccine that protects against chickenpox

virus—the smallest kind of germ. It can be seen only with a very powerful microscope.

white blood cell—a disease-fighting cell that travels in the blood and squeezes through the tiny gaps between cells in the body tissues

Learning More

Books

Brynie, Faith Hickman. *101 Questions About Your Skin That Got Under Your Skin Until Now.* New York: Twenty-First Century Books, 1999.

Kelley, True. *I've Got Chicken Pox.* New York: Dutton Children's Books, 1994.

Danziger, Paul. *You Can't Eat Your Chicken Pox.* New York: Apple, 1996.

Silverstein, Dr. Alvin, Virginia Silverstein, and Laura Silverstein Nunn. *Is that a Rash?* Danbury, CT: Franklin Watts, 1999.

Organizations and Online Sites

Chickenpox
http://www.health.state.ny.us/nysdoh/consumer/chickenp.htm
This site includes a fact sheet about chickenpox provided by the New York State Department of Health.

KidsHealth
http://kidshealth.org
This site features information about children's health for parents, kids, and teens.

The National Foundation for Infectious Diseases
4733 Bethesda Avenue, Ste. 750
Bethesda, MD 20814
http://www.nfid.org

National Institute of Allergy and Infectious Diseases
National Institutes of Health
9000 Rockville Pike, Bldg. 31
Bethesda, MD 20892
http://www.niaid.nih.gov/

VZV Research Foundation
40 East 72nd Street
New York, NY 10021
http://vzvfoundation.org/index.cfm

Index

Page numbers in *italics* indicate illustrations.

About the Authors

Dr. Alvin Silverstein is a professor of biology at the College of Staten Island of the City University of New York. **Virginia B. Silverstein** is a translator of Russian scientific literature. The Silversteins first worked together on a research project at the University of Pennsylvania. Since then, they have produced six children and more than 160 published books for young people.

Laura Silverstein Nunn, a graduate of Kean College, has been helping with her parents' books since her high school days. She is the coauthor of more than thirty books on diseases and health, science concepts, endangered species, and pets. Laura lives with her husband Matt and their young son Cory in a rural New Jersey town not far from her childhood home.